Rooted Issues: Digging Deeper to Discover the Real Issues of Your Heart - **second edition** book, Copyright © 2024 by Mayra Leon. All rights reserved for both the book and this *Rooted Issues Workbook*, the Cover design & all text by Mayra Leon Published in the United States of America, Copyright © 2024 by Mayra Leon. All rights reserved.

Rooted Issues Workbook

This workbook goes hand in hand with the book titled *Rooted Issues, second edition.*

This will help you face yourself and internal issues of the heart.

Questions & Exercises for personal growth or group studies
All of these are open for discussions.

<u>Introduction:</u>

What did you get from Janiece's story?

What was so important about you understanding the Introduction?

<u>Notes:</u>

<u>**Straight to the Root:**</u>

What was the point of Jesus talking to the Samaritan Woman at the well?

Why Samaria?

Why water?

<u>**Notes:**</u>

<u>**Facing your Past:**</u>

Based on the book, why is it important to face your past? Then tell why it is important <u>not</u> to continue looking back at your past & what Scripture is used for this one? (Two-part question)

-

-

<u>**Notes:**</u>

<u>Generational Curses:</u>

What is the main Chapter in Deuteronomy used for blessings and curses? _______________

Below is an exercise to break Generational Curses. You can even go as far as you remember with grandparents and so on. Write down the negative things you remember about your mother and then the ones about your father, letting the Holy Spirit lead you. Some examples could be illnesses, alcoholism, addictions, sexual perversions, abuse, abortions, divorce, controlling, passivity, adultery… Now start to break those things that you see in your own life that were passed down. Start to renounce (abandon, reject, surrender) and repent.

Some of you might struggle to find things, but some of you already know exactly what I am talking about and you can see it clearly. Start to pray against it. Stand in the gap for your parents and ask God to forgive them, as well as to forgive you. Renounce anything that you would have opened doors to against your generations to come (your children or grand-children). <u>Use a sheet of paper if you need extra space</u>. Break curses off of you and yours.

<u>Mother's Side</u>   <u>Father's Side</u>

<u>**Unforgiveness:**</u>

What is Matthew 18:21-35 and Matthew 6:14-15 really about?

In the book, what did the Author compare an old Roman punishment to? Describe it.

Now take a few sheets of paper (when I did this, I needed at least three sheets of paper). I want you to pray and ask God to show you names, faces, or events of people that you might still have unforgiveness towards. Only the Holy Spirit can reveal things of the heart. You may think you forgave someone already, but God will start bringing that person's face back up in your mind. It must be for a reason, so follow it and put that person's name down on that paper (just the name, not the whole story). You are going to make a list with the names, faces, or events that start to come up as you are praying for God to show you. An example of an event could be as such: You could have been raped and you cannot remember the face, nor ever knew their name; therefore, you can just write down the event—" rape." Some other examples could be a boss that fired you unjustly or a school teacher when you were younger who never liked you and treated you wrongly, someone who molested you, a neighbor who is annoying you, a friend who stole your lover or a bully from your past. You might even have to forgive your son or daughter who has stolen from you, mistreats you or has lied to you over and over again. I could go on and on, but the bottom line is that you have to make this list under the power and direction of the Holy Spirit revealing these people to you.

Once the list is complete, go back to number one. Note, the first three on your list are usually the hardest to deal with. When you start with number one, present this person or event to the Lord. Talk to God about what took place and then let God know that you choose to forgive that person. <u>Please do not just do a general prayer over your entire</u>

<u>paper because it is more effective if you take the time to look at each episode of your life again and deal with it **one at a time**</u>.

Cry, scream, punch a pillow if you have to, but know that God is right there with you to walk you through this. You might even want to put a chair in front of you, as though that person is sitting there in front of you.

You may even want to have someone there with you to coach you along. Make sure this individual is godly minded and positive. Also, make sure that you trust them with your personal issues.

As you talk to God about **each one**, finish by stating that you will close this chapter of your life and that you apply the Blood of Jesus over it, never to open it again. When you reach the end, take the paper and burn it or just rip it into little pieces. Throw it out. You can even turn it into a prayer list so you can pray for them. This might take you one day or maybe a few days; However long it takes, make sure that you don't leave anyone off your list without dealing with it. You might have to forgive every day, such as your spouse, but still know that if that is what it takes, then die daily to your will and emotions and do it for God first and then for yourself. Don't forget that you might have to forgive yourself first. You might even be angry with God; this is a good time to deal with this matter. He is always willing to forgive you.

As soon as you are done with this list, know for sure that the devil will not be happy about it, so he will try to instigate by using someone from that list to call you and start trouble or for a family member to call you and remind you of your past. Whatever the case may be, know that your enemy doesn't want to see you free. Don't let yourself get inside the web again. First Peter 5:8–11 tells us, that the enemy roams around like a lion seeking whom he may devour. Be alert! Remember that forgiveness is for you!

<u>Extra Notes:</u>

<u>Rebellion</u>:

Why does the Author use the story of the Roman Soldier and the importance of submitting to authority, not just having faith? Where in the Bible is that story found?

What is the Author's own definition of Rebellion, according to what's in the book?

Rebellion is like the sin of ____.

Obedience is better than ____________________. What Scripture is this? ______________

What's the Author's issue with the seat belt and why does she say that story?

What was so important about Judges 2:20-23?

The Scripture of Galatians 6:9 says:

Ecclesiastes 12:13–14 says:

What does Messiah mean and what language is it in?

What does Christ mean and what language is it in?

Give the English translation of both.

<u>Notes:</u>

Your mouth, ears and eyes are ________________________.

What are some of the different ways the mouth can operate in a negative way based on the book?

-
-
-
-
-

Ephesians 4:29 says

What was the parable of "the chocolate donut" dealing with in this chapter (not weight)?

Matthew 12:36– 37 says?

Proverbs 18 – what **verse** says that you have the power of life or death in your tongue?
____

What happens when you allow *negative* talk or music through the ear gates, based on the book?

What happens when you allow *negative* pictures/movies through the eye gates based on the book?

Read James 3:1-12

Notes:

<u>**Rejection**</u>:

What is the point of the story with the woman who saw a vision of a mother delivering a baby and calling the baby "IT"?

Based on the chapter, what does rejection also come with? (Give approximately 7 things).

1.

2.

3.

4.

5.

6.

7.

See the list of "*Who I Am In Christ*" in the back of this workbook. This list is important to do every day for at least 21 days to renew your mind.

Why 21 days? (based on what the author said in the book)

Started the list today; Date: _______________________
Date of 21 days later _________________

<u>Witchcraft/Occult</u>:

When you use witchcraft/occult, what would be some of the outcomes per the book?

What is Necromancy? Give 3 Scriptures that were used against it.

-

-

-

Give some examples of <u>subtle</u> witchcraft from the book:

What was the Author's experience after she was saved regarding Astrology?

Who was Jezebel in the Bible and name one or two of her characteristics mentioned in the book?

In the Bible, the book of Revelation 2:20 talks about what?

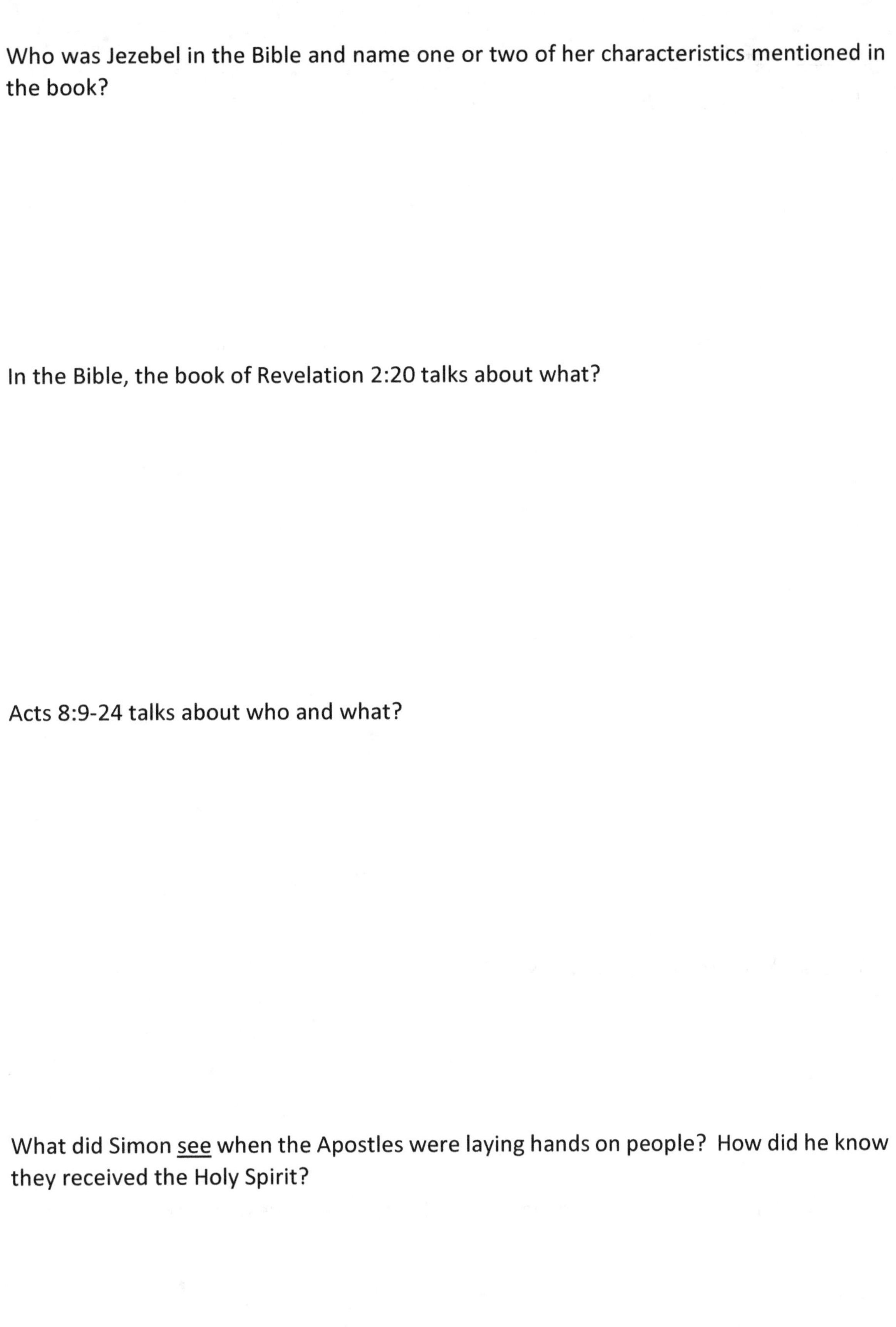

Acts 8:9-24 talks about who and what?

What did Simon <u>see</u> when the Apostles were laying hands on people? How did he know they received the Holy Spirit?

<u>**Sexual Immorality:**</u>

What was the point of Jeremiah 3:2-5 in the book?

In short, what happened to the Author when she battled with adultery?

Why couldn't she go back to reading the Bible for herself right away?

1 Thessalonians 4:1–8 talks about what?

What are demons that are called Incubus (male) and Succubus (female)?

Sometimes we have to admit in order to get help. It's the truth that sets you free! Yes, we must love the sinner, but not the sin. In the Bible, Romans 1:24–32 talks about what?

Pray and check to see if there are articles in your house that need to be removed, things that draw in perverted demons: such as perversion in movies and music, sexual clothing, porn items, pictures of such, artifacts geared to perversion, things you listen to or watch, and so on. Even if you don't have these things visibly, someone in your household may have them hidden. Pray and be led by the Holy Spirit to help you find them. Once you find them, get rid of them in a fire or trash where you can't go back to them or for anyone else to fine. Be obedient for your own good and the good of your family. Did you find something?

<u>Notes:</u>

<u>**Ungodly Soul ties:**</u>

We are made of 3 parts: ___________________, ___________________, &
___________________.

The soul consists of your ___________________, ___________________, &
___________________.

Soul ties don't have to be just sexual; give at least 4 short examples of such, from the book:

Ephesians 5:31 says?

The Author took a Christmas trip with her family; what happened during that trip regarding her children?

What happened to Jonathan, the Author's son?

What happened to the Author's husband right after Jonathan?

Luke 9:62 says?

The following is an exercise to break or divorce ungodly soul ties: Be led by the Holy Spirit through prayer. Ask God and take a sheet of paper, make a list, and do the same thing you did for the chapter of unforgiveness, only this time, you will ask God to show you the ungodly soul ties you may still have.

Think back to the first person who took your virginity, then write down all the people you had sex with (if you can't remember them all, just put on one of the lines, "the ones I can't remember"). God knows the heart and God knows who they are.

After those people, go to the ones that are ungodly soul ties outside of sex, such as Mom or Dad, friendships that are hard to break, a death of a pet or loved one—an ungodly soul tie can even be a house that you've lived in for years and may carry certain memories, or a certain city that you will not move out of, a job or even an item (jewelry, clothing and such).

After you finish your list, go back to number one and start to divorce them (from your soul) one at a time or cutting the ties. Ask God to sever people or things. Do not do a general prayer because it is more effective if you do this one at a time.

Also, in this Chapter, the Author explains about a Conference and how the Lord led her to speak about releasing the adult children and grandchildren. Then she asked them to put the names of their adult children and grandchildren on a sheet of paper and to begin confessing that they would release them to God and that they would no longer control or worry (fear) over them with God's help. Please do that now and begin to let go, because we have to trust God and His love for them, which is greater than ours.

Once you are all done, <u>rip all the pages</u>. Close those chapters of your life, never to open them again. You might need to ask God to forgive you for not trusting Him and for not allowing yourself to let go.

I know problems are not solved just by ripping them up on paper; however, it is a mirror and the beginning of a new you. This is not in vain and God will meet you.

<u>Notes:</u>

<u>**Enlarging Your Territory**</u>

In a few words, what is the prayer of Jabez and where is it found in the Bible?

What did the Author mean by enlarging her territory?

What was the issue with Matthew 20:21–27 and Mark 10:35 in the Bible?

Use wisdom when you ask God for something, because it may cost a heavy price.

Give at least 4 ways God enlarged the Author's territory:

1.

2.

3.

4.

<u>Notes:</u>

<u>**Heart, Faith & Grace**</u>

What is the account in Luke 23:39-43, Bible:

What did the thief on the Cross do to deserve going with Jesus to Paradise (Kingdom)?

John 6:28-29 says:

Jeremiah 31:15-20 talks about what?

Matthew 7:3-5 talks about what?

Can you name some people in the Bible that have died tragically? Not the evil ones.

Matthew 18:11-14 (NKJV) says?

Give a <u>short</u> summary of this Chapter in your own words. Please include heart, faith & Grace:

<u>**Anger**</u>

Proverbs 25:28 says?

Name at least 6 things that can come in with anger: ________________,
________________, ________________, ________________,
________________, ________________

Anger is a product of a ________________________ ________________.

Why was the lady in the store battling with rooted anger?

After that whole ordeal, the Author learned a very valuable lesson, what was it?

Why do you battle anger? Ask God now to reveal to you the root of the anger. Let yourself become vulnerable for Him to show you. Repent, forgive and ask God now to heal you and yank the root. Don't be afraid.

<u>**Fears**</u>

What is the Scripture used to conquer the Strong Man first?

Why does the Author mention Goliath and the antagonist in movies - Main point?

Give <u>5</u> different kinds of fears and at least <u>3</u> ways to conquer them.

1.

2.

3.

4.

5.

1.

2.

3.

Briefly tell why the Author mentions 2 Chronicles chapter 20.

For those who may think that the following list is unreal or far-fetched, know that the Author has met people with these types of fears and they are very real. In fact, someone dear to the Author's heart, had a fear of stickers and would throw up and scream if they would try to put it on that person or even come close with stickers or tape.

FEAR – Phobia LIST: (This is a list found online**)**

Ablutophobia- Fear of washing or bathing.
Acarophobia- Fear of itching or of the insects that cause itching.
Acerophobia- Fear of sourness.
Achluophobia- Fear of darkness.
Acousticophobia- Fear of noise.
Acrophobia- Fear of heights.
Aerophobia- Fear of drafts, air swallowing, or airbourne noxious substances.
Aeroacrophobia- Fear of open high places.
Aeronausiphobia- Fear of vomiting secondary to air sickness.
Agateophobia- Fear of insanity.
Agliophobia- Fear of pain.
Agoraphobia- Fear of open spaces or of being in crowded, public places like markets. Fear of leaving a safe place.
Agraphobia- Fear of sexual abuse.
Agrizoophobia- Fear of wild animals.
Agyrophobia- Fear of streets or crossing the street.
Aichmophobia- Fear of needles or pointed objects.
Ailurophobia- Fear of cats.
Albuminurophobia- Fear of kidney disease.
Alektorophobia- Fear of chickens.
Algophobia- Fear of pain.
Alliumphobia- Fear of garlic.
Allodoxaphobia- Fear of opinions.
Altophobia- Fear of heights.
Amathophobia- Fear of dust.

Amaxophobia- Fear of riding in a car.
Ambulophobia- Fear of walking.
Amnesiphobia- Fear of amnesia.
Amychophobia- Fear of scratches or being scratched.
Anablephobia- Fear of looking up.
Ancraophobia- Fear of wind. (Anemophobia)
Androphobia- Fear of men.
Anemophobia- Fear of air drafts or wind. (Ancraophobia)
Anginophobia- Fear of angina, choking or narrowness.
Anglophobia- Fear of England or English culture, etc.
Angrophobia - Fear of anger or of becoming angry.
Ankylophobia- Fear of immobility of a joint.
Anthrophobia or Anthophobia- Fear of flowers.
Anthropophobia- Fear of people or society.

Antlophobia- Fear of floods.
Anuptaphobia- Fear of staying single.
Apeirophobia- Fear of infinity.
Aphenphosmphobia- Fear of being touched. (Haphephobia)
Apiphobia- Fear of bees.
Apotemnophobia- Fear of persons with amputations.
Arachibutyrophobia- Fear of peanut butter sticking to the roof of the mouth.
Arachnephobia or Arachnophobia- Fear of spiders.
Arithmophobia- Fear of numbers.
Arrhenphobia- Fear of men.
Arsonphobia- Fear of fire.
Asthenophobia- Fear of fainting or weakness.
Astraphobia or Astrapophobia- Fear of thunder and lightning.(Ceraunophobia, Keraunophobia)
Astrophobia- Fear of stars or celestial space.
Asymmetriphobia- Fear of asymmetrical things.
Ataxiophobia- Fear of ataxia. (muscular incoordination)
Ataxophobia- Fear of disorder or untidiness.
Atelophobia- Fear of imperfection.
Atephobia- Fear of ruin or ruins.
Athazagoraphobia- Fear of being forgotton or ignored or forgetting.
Atomosophobia- Fear of atomic explosions.
Atychiphobia- Fear of failure.
Aulophobia- Fear of flutes.
Aurophobia- Fear of gold.
Auroraphobia- Fear of Northern lights.
Autodysomophobia- Fear of one that has a vile odor.
Automatonophobia- Fear of ventriloquist's dummies, animatronic creatures, wax statues - anything that falsly represents a sentient being.
Automysophobia- Fear of being dirty.

Autophobia- Fear of being alone or of oneself.
Aviophobia or Aviatophobia- Fear of flying.

Bacillophobia- Fear of microbes.
Bacteriophobia- Fear of bacteria.
Ballistophobia- Fear of missiles or bullets.
Bolshephobia- Fear of Bolsheviks.
Barophobia- Fear of gravity.
Basophobia or Basiphobia- Inability to stand. Fear of walking or falling.
Bathmophobia- Fear of stairs or steep slopes.
Bathophobia- Fear of depth.
Batophobia- Fear of heights or being close to high buildings.
Batrachophobia- Fear of amphibians, such as frogs, newts, salamanders, etc.
Belonephobia- Fear of pins and needles. (Aichmophobia)
Bibliophobia- Fear of books.
Blennophobia- Fear of slime.
Bogyphobia- Fear of bogeys or the bogeyman.
Botanophobia- Fear of plants.
Bromidrosiphobia or Bromidrophobia- Fear of body smells.
Brontophobia- Fear of thunder and lightning.
Bufonophobia- Fear of toads.

Cacophobia- Fear of ugliness.
Cainophobia or Cainotophobia- Fear of newness, novelty.
Caligynephobia- Fear of beautiful women.
Cancerophobia or Carcinophobia- Fear of cancer.
Cardiophobia- Fear of the heart.
Carnophobia- Fear of meat.
Catagelophobia- Fear of being ridiculed.
Catapedaphobia- Fear of jumping from high and low places.
Cathisophobia- Fear of sitting.
Catoptrophobia- Fear of mirrors.
Cenophobia or Centophobia- Fear of new things or ideas.
Ceraunophobia or Keraunophobia- Fear of thunder and lightning.(Astraphobia, Astrapophobia)
Chaetophobia- Fear of hair.
Cheimaphobia or Cheimatophobia- Fear of cold.(Frigophobia, Psychophobia)
Chemophobia- Fear of chemicals or working with chemicals.
Cherophobia- Fear of gaiety.
Chionophobia- Fear of snow.
Chiraptophobia- Fear of being touched.
Chirophobia- Fear of hands.
Chiroptophobia- Fear of bats.
Cholerophobia- Fear of anger or the fear of cholera.
Chorophobia- Fear of dancing.
Chrometophobia or Chrematophobia- Fear of money.

Chromophobia or Chromatophobia- Fear of colors.
Chronophobia- Fear of time.
Chronomentrophobia- Fear of clocks.
Cibophobia- Fear of food.(Sitophobia, Sitiophobia)
Claustrophobia- Fear of confined spaces.
Cleithrophobia or Cleisiophobia- Fear of being locked in an enclosed place.
Cleptophobia- Fear of stealing.
Climacophobia- Fear of stairs, climbing, or of falling downstairs.
Clinophobia- Fear of going to bed.
Clithrophobia or Cleithrophobia- Fear of being enclosed.
Cnidophobia- Fear of stings.
Cometophobia- Fear of comets.
Coimetrophobia- Fear of cemeteries.
Coitophobia- Fear of coitus.
Contreltophobia- Fear of sexual abuse.
Coprastasophobia- Fear of constipation.
Coprophobia- Fear of feces.
Consecotaleophobia- Fear of chopsticks.
Coulrophobia- Fear of clowns.
Counterphobia- The preference by a phobic for fearful situations.
Cremnophobia- Fear of precipices.
Cryophobia- Fear of extreme cold, ice or frost.
Crystallophobia- Fear of crystals or glass.
Cyberphobia- Fear of computers or working on a computer.
Cyclophobia- Fear of bicycles.
Cymophobia or Kymophobia- Fear of waves or wave like motions.
Cynophobia- Fear of dogs or rabies.
Cypridophobia or Cypriphobia or Cyprianophobia or Cyprinophobia - Fear of prostitutes or venereal disease.

Decidophobia- Fear of making decisions.
Defecaloesiophobia- Fear of painful bowels movements.
Deipnophobia- Fear of dining or dinner conversations.
Dementophobia- Fear of insanity.
Demonophobia or Daemonophobia- Fear of demons.
Demophobia- Fear of crowds. (Agoraphobia)
Dendrophobia- Fear of trees.
Dentophobia- Fear of dentists.
Dermatophobia- Fear of skin lesions.
Dermatosiophobia or Dermatophobia or Dermatopathophobia- Fear of skin disease.
Dextrophobia- Fear of objects at the right side of the body.
Diabetophobia- Fear of diabetes.
Didaskaleinophobia- Fear of going to school.
Dikephobia- Fear of justice.
Dinophobia- Fear of dizziness or whirlpools.
Diplophobia- Fear of double vision.
Dipsophobia- Fear of drinking.

Dishabiliophobia- Fear of undressing in front of someone.
Disposophobia- Fear of throwing stuff out. Hoarding.
Domatophobia- Fear of houses or being in a house. (Eicophobia, Oikophobia)
Doraphobia- Fear of fur or skins of animals.
Doxophobia- Fear of expressing opinions or of receiving praise.
Dromophobia- Fear of crossing streets.
Dutchphobia- Fear of the Dutch.
Dysmorphophobia- Fear of deformity.
Dystychiphobia- Fear of accidents.

Ecclesiophobia- Fear of church.
Ecophobia- Fear of home.
Eicophobia- Fear of home surroundings. (Domatophobia, Oikophobia)
Eisoptrophobia- Fear of mirrors or of seeing oneself in a mirror.
Electrophobia- Fear of electricity.
Eleutherophobia- Fear of freedom.
Elurophobia- Fear of cats. (Ailurophobia)
Emetophobia- Fear of vomiting.
Enetophobia- Fear of pins.
Enochlophobia- Fear of crowds.
Enosiophobia or Enissophobia- Fear of having committed an unpardonable sin or of criticism.
Entomophobia- Fear of insects.
Eosophobia- Fear of dawn or daylight.
Ephebiphobia- Fear of teenagers.
Epistaxiophobia- Fear of nosebleeds.
Epistemophobia- Fear of knowledge.
Equinophobia- Fear of horses.
Eremophobia- Fear of being oneself or of lonliness.
Ereuthrophobia- Fear of blushing.
Ergasiophobia- 1) Fear of work or functioning. 2) Surgeon's fear of operating.
Ergophobia- Fear of work.
Erotophobia- Fear of sexual love or sexual questions.
Euphobia- Fear of hearing good news.
Eurotophobia- Fear of female genitalia.
Erythrophobia or Erytophobia or Ereuthophobia- 1) Fear of redlights. 2) Blushing. 3) Red.

Febriphobia or Fibriphobia or Fibriophobia- Fear of fever.
Felinophobia- Fear of cats. (Ailurophobia, Elurophobia, Galeophobia, Gatophobia)
Francophobia- Fear of France or French culture. (Gallophobia, Galiophobia)
Frigophobia- Fear of cold or cold things. (Cheimaphobia, Cheimatophobia, Psychrophobia)

Galeophobia or Gatophobia- Fear of cats.
Gallophobia or Galiophobia- Fear France or French culture. (Francophobia)
Gamophobia- Fear of marriage.
Geliophobia- Fear of laughter.
Gelotophobia- Fear of being laughed at.
Geniophobia- Fear of chins.
Genophobia- Fear of sex.
Genuphobia- Fear of knees.
Gephyrophobia or Gephydrophobia or Gephysrophobia- Fear of crossing bridges.
Germanophobia- Fear of Germany or German culture.
Gerascophobia- Fear of growing old.
Gerontophobia- Fear of old people or of growing old.
Geumaphobia or Geumophobia- Fear of taste.
Glossophobia- Fear of speaking in public or of trying to speak.
Gnosiophobia- Fear of knowledge.
Graphophobia- Fear of writing or handwriting.
Gymnophobia- Fear of nudity.
Gynephobia or Gynophobia- Fear of women.

Hadephobia- Fear of hell.
Hagiophobia- Fear of saints or holy things.
Hamartophobia- Fear of sinning.
Haphephobia or Haptephobia- Fear of being touched.
Harpaxophobia- Fear of being robbed.
Hedonophobia- Fear of feeling pleasure.
Heliophobia- Fear of the sun.
Hellenologophobia- Fear of Greek terms or complex scientific terminology.
Helminthophobia- Fear of being infested with worms.
Hemophobia or Hemaphobia or Hematophobia- Fear of blood.
Heresyphobia or Hereiophobia- Fear of challenges to official doctrine or
of radical deviation.
Herpetophobia- Fear of reptiles or creepy, crawly things.
Heterophobia- Fear of the opposite sex. (Sexophobia)
Hexakosioihexekontahexaphobia- Fear of the number 666.
Hierophobia- Fear of priests or sacred things.
Hippophobia- Fear of horses.
Hippopotomonstrosesquipedaliophobia- Fear of long words.
Hobophobia- Fear of bums or beggars.
Hodophobia- Fear of road travel.
Hormephobia- Fear of shock.
Homichlophobia- Fear of fog.
Homilophobia- Fear of sermons.
Hominophobia- Fear of men.
Homophobia- Fear of sameness, monotony or of homosexuality or of becoming
homosexual.

Hoplophobia- Fear of firearms.
Hydrargyophobia- Fear of mercurial medicines.
Hydrophobia- Fear of water or of rabies.
Hydrophobophobia- Fear of rabies.
Hyelophobia or Hyalophobia- Fear of glass.
Hygrophobia- Fear of liquids, dampness, or moisture.
Hylephobia- Fear of materialism or the fear of epilepsy.
Hylophobia- Fear of forests.
Hypengyophobia or Hypegiaphobia- Fear of responsibility.
Hypnophobia- Fear of sleep or of being hypnotized.
Hypsiphobia- Fear of height.

Iatrophobia- Fear of going to the doctor or of doctors.
Ichthyophobia- Fear of fish.
Ideophobia- Fear of ideas.
Illyngophobia- Fear of vertigo or feeling dizzy when looking down.
Iophobia- Fear of poison.
Insectophobia - Fear of insects.
Isolophobia- Fear of solitude, being alone.
Isopterophobia- Fear of termites, insects that eat wood.
Ithyphallophobia- Fear of seeing, thinking about or having an erect penis.

Japanophobia- Fear of Japanese.
Judeophobia- Fear of Jews.

Kainolophobia or Kainophobia- Fear of anything new, novelty.
Kakorrhaphiophobia- Fear of failure or defeat.
Katagelophobia- Fear of ridicule.
Kathisophobia- Fear of sitting down.
Katsaridaphobia- Fear of cockroaches.
Kenophobia- Fear of voids or empty spaces.
Keraunophobia or Ceraunophobia- Fear of thunder and lightning.(Astraphobia, Astrapophobia)
Kinetophobia or Kinesophobia- Fear of movement or motion.
Kleptophobia- Fear of stealing.
Koinoniphobia- Fear of rooms.
Kolpophobia- Fear of genitals, particularly female.
Kopophobia- Fear of fatigue.
Koniophobia- Fear of dust. (Amathophobia)
Kosmikophobia- Fear of cosmic phenomenon.
Kymophobia- Fear of waves. (Cymophobia)
Kynophobia- Fear of rabies.
Kyphophobia- Fear of stooping.

Lachanophobia- Fear of vegetables.
Laliophobia or Lalophobia- Fear of speaking.

Leprophobia or Lepraphobia- Fear of leprosy.
Leukophobia- Fear of the color white.
Levophobia- Fear of things to the left side of the body.
Ligyrophobia- Fear of loud noises.
Lilapsophobia- Fear of tornadoes and hurricanes.
Limnophobia- Fear of lakes.
Linonophobia- Fear of string.
Liticaphobia- Fear of lawsuits.
Lockiophobia- Fear of childbirth.
Logizomechanophobia- Fear of computers.
Logophobia- Fear of words.
Luiphobia- Fear of lues, syphillis.
Lutraphobia- Fear of otters.
Lygophobia- Fear of darkness.
Lyssophobia- Fear of rabies or of becoming mad.

Macrophobia- Fear of long waits.
Mageirocophobia- Fear of cooking.
Maieusiophobia- Fear of childbirth.
Malaxophobia- Fear of love play. (Sarmassophobia)
Maniaphobia- Fear of insanity.
Mastigophobia- Fear of punishment.
Mechanophobia- Fear of machines.
Medomalacuphobia- Fear of losing an erection.
Medorthophobia- Fear of an erect penis.
Megalophobia- Fear of large things.
Melissophobia- Fear of bees.
Melanophobia- Fear of the color black.
Melophobia- Fear or hatred of music.
Meningitophobia- Fear of brain disease.
Menophobia- Fear of menstruation.
Merinthophobia- Fear of being bound or tied up.
Metallophobia- Fear of metal.
Metathesiophobia- Fear of changes.
Meteorophobia- Fear of meteors.
Methyphobia- Fear of alcohol.
Metrophobia- Fear or hatred of poetry.
Microbiophobia- Fear of microbes. (Bacillophobia)
Microphobia- Fear of small things.
Misophobia or Mysophobia- Fear of being contaminated with dirt or germs.
Mnemophobia- Fear of memories.
Molysmophobia or Molysomophobia- Fear of dirt or contamination.
Monophobia- Fear of solitude or being alone.
Monopathophobia- Fear of definite disease.
Motorphobia- Fear of automobiles.

Mottephobia- Fear of moths.
Musophobia or Muriphobia- Fear of mice.
Mycophobia- Fear or aversion to mushrooms.
Mycrophobia- Fear of small things.
Myctophobia- Fear of darkness.
Myrmecophobia- Fear of ants.
Mythophobia- Fear of myths or stories or false statements.
Myxophobia- Fear of slime. (Blennophobia)

Nebulaphobia- Fear of fog. (Homichlophobia)
Necrophobia- Fear of death or dead things.
Nelophobia- Fear of glass.
Neopharmaphobia- Fear of new drugs.
Neophobia- Fear of anything new.
Nephophobia- Fear of clouds.
Noctiphobia- Fear of the night.
Nomatophobia- Fear of names.
Nosocomephobia- Fear of hospitals.
Nosophobia or Nosemaphobia- Fear of becoming ill.
Nostophobia- Fear of returning home.
Novercaphobia- Fear of your step-mother.
Nucleomituphobia- Fear of nuclear weapons.
Nudophobia- Fear of nudity.
Numerophobia- Fear of numbers.
Nyctohylophobia- Fear of dark wooded areas or of forests at night
Nyctophobia- Fear of the dark or of night.

Obesophobia- Fear of gaining weight. (Pocrescophobia)
Ochlophobia- Fear of crowds or mobs.
Ochophobia- Fear of vehicles.
Octophobia - Fear of the figure 8.
Odontophobia- Fear of teeth or dental surgery.
Odynophobia or Odynephobia- Fear of pain. (Algophobia)
Oenophobia- Fear of wines.
Oikophobia- Fear of home surroundings, house. (Domatophobia, Eicophobia)
Olfactophobia- Fear of smells.
Ombrophobia- Fear of rain or of being rained on.
Ommetaphobia or Ommatophobia- Fear of eyes.
Omphalophobia- Fear of belly buttons.
Oneirophobia- Fear of dreams.
Oneirogmophobia- Fear of wet dreams.
Onomatophobia- Fear of hearing a certain word or of names.
Ophidiophobia- Fear of snakes. (Snakephobia)
Ophthalmophobia- Fear of being stared at.
Opiophobia- Fear medical doctors experience of prescribing needed pain

medications for patients.
Optophobia- Fear of opening one's eyes.
Ornithophobia- Fear of birds.
Orthophobia- Fear of property.
Osmophobia or Osphresiophobia- Fear of smells or odors.
Ostraconophobia- Fear of shellfish.
Ouranophobia or Uranophobia- Fear of heaven.

Pagophobia- Fear of ice or frost.
Panthophobia- Fear of suffering and disease.
Panophobia or Pantophobia- Fear of everything.
Papaphobia- Fear of the Pope.
Papyrophobia- Fear of paper.
Paralipophobia- Fear of neglecting duty or responsibility.
Paraphobia- Fear of sexual perversion.
Parasitophobia- Fear of parasites.
Paraskavedekatriaphobia- Fear of Friday the 13th.
Parthenophobia- Fear of virgins or young girls.
Pathophobia- Fear of disease.
Patroiophobia- Fear of heredity.
Parturiphobia- Fear of childbirth.
Peccatophobia- Fear of sinning or imaginary crimes.
Pediculophobia- Fear of lice.
Pediophobia- Fear of dolls.
Pedophobia- Fear of children.
Peladophobia- Fear of bald people.
Pellagrophobia- Fear of pellagra.
Peniaphobia- Fear of poverty.
Pentheraphobia- Fear of mother-in-law. (Novercaphobia)
Phagophobia- Fear of swallowing or of eating or of being eaten.
Phalacrophobia- Fear of becoming bald.
Phallophobia- Fear of a penis, esp erect.
Pharmacophobia- Fear of taking medicine.
Phasmophobia- Fear of ghosts.
Phengophobia- Fear of daylight or sunshine.
Philemaphobia or Philematophobia- Fear of kissing.
Philophobia- Fear of falling in love or being in love.
Philosophobia- Fear of philosophy.
Phobophobia- Fear of phobias.
Photoaugliaphobia- Fear of glaring lights.
Photophobia- Fear of light.
Phonophobia- Fear of noises or voices or one's own voice; of telephones.
Phronemophobia- Fear of thinking.
Phthiriophobia- Fear of lice. (Pediculophobia)
Phthisiophobia- Fear of tuberculosis.

Placophobia- Fear of tombstones.
Plutophobia- Fear of wealth.
Pluviophobia- Fear of rain or of being rained on.
Pneumatiphobia- Fear of spirits.
Pnigophobia or Pnigerophobia- Fear of choking of being smothered.
Pocrescophobia- Fear of gaining weight. (Obesophobia)
Pogonophobia- Fear of beards.
Poliosophobia- Fear of contracting poliomyelitis.
Politicophobia- Fear or abnormal dislike of politicians.
Polyphobia- Fear of many things.
Poinephobia- Fear of punishment.
Ponophobia- Fear of overworking or of pain.
Porphyrophobia- Fear of the color purple.
Potamophobia- Fear of rivers or running water.
Potophobia- Fear of alcohol.
Pharmacophobia- Fear of drugs.
Proctophobia- Fear of rectums.
Prosophobia- Fear of progress.
Psellismophobia- Fear of stuttering.
Psychophobia- Fear of mind.
Psychrophobia- Fear of cold.
Pteromerhanophobia- Fear of flying.
Pteronophobia- Fear of being tickled by feathers.
Pupaphobia - Fear of puppets.
Pyrexiophobia- Fear of Fever.
Pyrophobia- Fear of fire.

Radiophobia- Fear of radiation, x-rays.
Ranidaphobia- Fear of frogs.
Rectophobia- Fear of rectum or rectal diseases.
Rhabdophobia- Fear of being severely punished or beaten by a rod, or of being severely criticized. Also fear of magic. (wand)
Rhypophobia- Fear of defecation.
Rhytiphobia- Fear of getting wrinkles.
Rupophobia- Fear of dirt.
Russophobia- Fear of Russians.

Samhainophobia: Fear of Halloween.
Sarmassophobia- Fear of love play. (Malaxophobia)
Satanophobia- Fear of Satan.
Scabiophobia- Fear of scabies.
Scatophobia- Fear of fecal matter.
Scelerophibia- Fear of bad men, burglars.
Sciophobia Sciaphobia- Fear of shadows.
Scoleciphobia- Fear of worms.
Scolionophobia- Fear of school.

Scopophobia or Scoptophobia- Fear of being seen or stared at.
Scotomaphobia- Fear of blindness in visual field.
Scotophobia- Fear of darkness. (Achluophobia)
Scriptophobia- Fear of writing in public.
Selachophobia- Fear of sharks.
Selaphobia- Fear of light flashes.
Selenophobia- Fear of the moon.
Seplophobia- Fear of decaying matter.
Sesquipedalophobia- Fear of long words.
Sexophobia- Fear of the opposite sex. (Heterophobia)
Siderodromophobia- Fear of trains, railroads or train travel.
Siderophobia- Fear of stars.
Sinistrophobia- Fear of things to the left or left-handed.
Sinophobia- Fear of Chinese, Chinese culture.
Sitophobia or Sitiophobia- Fear of food or eating. (Cibophobia)
Snakephobia- Fear of snakes. (Ophidiophobia)
Soceraphobia- Fear of parents-in-law.
Social Phobia- Fear of being evaluated negatively in social situations.
Sociophobia- Fear of society or people in general.
Somniphobia- Fear of sleep.
Sophophobia- Fear of learning.
Soteriophobia - Fear of dependence on others.
Spacephobia- Fear of outer space.
Spectrophobia- Fear of specters or ghosts.
Spermatophobia or Spermophobia- Fear of germs.
Spheksophobia- Fear of wasps.
Stasibasiphobia or Stasiphobia- Fear of standing or walking. (Ambulophobia)
Staurophobia- Fear of crosses or the crucifix.
Stenophobia- Fear of narrow things or places.
Stygiophobia or Stigiophobia- Fear of hell.
Suriphobia- Fear of mice.
Symbolophobia- Fear of symbolism.
Symmetrophobia- Fear of symmetry.
Syngenesophobia- Fear of relatives.
Syphilophobia- Fear of syphilis.

Tachophobia- Fear of speed.
Taeniophobia or Teniophobia- Fear of tapeworms.
Taphephobia Taphophobia- Fear of being buried alive or of cemeteries.
Tapinophobia- Fear of being contagious.
Taurophobia- Fear of bulls.
Technophobia- Fear of technology.
Teleophobia- 1) Fear of definite plans. 2) Religious ceremony.
Telephonophobia- Fear of telephones.
Teratophobia- Fear of bearing a deformed child or fear of monsters or deformed people.
Testophobia- Fear of taking tests.

Tetanophobia- Fear of lockjaw, tetanus.
Teutophobia- Fear of German or German things.
Textophobia- Fear of certain fabrics.
Thaasophobia- Fear of sitting.
Thalassophobia- Fear of the sea.
Thanatophobia or Thantophobia- Fear of death or dying.
Theatrophobia- Fear of theatres.
Theologicophobia- Fear of theology.
Theophobia- Fear of gods or religion.
Thermophobia- Fear of heat.
Tocophobia- Fear of pregnancy or childbirth.
Tomophobia- Fear of surgical operations.
Tonitrophobia- Fear of thunder.
Topophobia- Fear of certain places or situations, such as stage fright.
Toxiphobia or Toxophobia or Toxicophobia- Fear of poison or of being accidently poisoned.
Traumatophobia- Fear of injury.
Tremophobia- Fear of trembling.
Trichinophobia- Fear of trichinosis.
Trichopathophobia or Trichophobia- Fear of hair. (Chaetophobia, Hypertrichophobia)
Triskaidekaphobia- Fear of the number 13.
Tropophobia- Fear of moving or making changes.
Trypanophobia- Fear of injections.
Tuberculophobia- Fear of tuberculosis.
Tyrannophobia- Fear of tyrants.

Uranophobia or Ouranophobia- Fear of Heaven.
Urophobia- Fear of urine or urinating.

Vaccinophobia- Fear of vaccination.
Venustraphobia- Fear of beautiful women.
Verbophobia- Fear of words.
Verminophobia- Fear of germs.
Vestiphobia- Fear of clothing.
Virginitiphobia- Fear of rape.
Vitricophobia- Fear of step-father.

Walloonphobia- Fear of the Walloons.
Wiccaphobia: Fear of witches and witchcraft

Xanthophobia- Fear of the color yellow or the word yellow.
Xenoglossophobia- Fear of foreign languages.
Xenophobia- Fear of strangers or foreigners.
Xerophobia- Fear of dryness.
Xylophobia- 1) Fear of wooden objects. 2) Forests.
Xyrophobia-Fear of razors.

Zelophobia- Fear of jealousy.
Zeusophobia- Fear of gods.
Zemmiphobia- Fear of the great mole rat.
Zoophobia- Fear of animals.

Pray against any fears that you or your family battle. Use the Word of God (The Sword of the Spirit) against them. Face them, go through it, even if you're afraid. Whatever you do, don't stay stuck, don't run away, confront and God will be with you through it. You will overcome; Have Faith and Trust God that He will help you. Like a good Father, He will never leave you.

1 John 4:4 says?

What fears have you overcome by confronting them?

Pray that God would give you boldness and help you to overcome and confront.

Read Psalm 91

Notes:

<u>**Nakedness**</u>

In the second and third paragraphs, it talks about Covering. Below, give a few points from those two paragraphs.

2nd Paragraph -

3rd Paragraph –

Why Psalm 91 for those 2 paragraphs?

Why did Adam cover himself with leaves?

Based on why Adam covered himself, what can sin bring? Name just a few.

_____________________, _____________________, _____________________,
____

Who does Noah curse and who does he bless based on the account in the Bible in Genesis
9:18–27?

Not literal nakedness, but what is the Author referring to when she talks about nakedness?

What is the Author talking about when she mentions "a private in the military trying to correct a general or a student in school trying to correct the principal."?

We don't condone, but 1 Peter 4:8 says?

Notes:

<u>**Pride/Haughtiness**</u>

Proverbs 6:16–19 - What are at least 6 things the Lord despises?

1.

2.

3.

4.

5.

6.

King Nebuchadnezzar is an example of pride in Daniel 4:28 -37, why? Give a few details as to what happened to him and how long before he was restored:

Why is Humpty-Dumpty mentioned in this Chapter?

What is the "what about me?" syndrome:

What is a narcissist?

What is the <u>main point</u> of the parable in Luke 18:9–14?

Proverbs 16:18-19 says:

Ask God where this root of pride came from. Could it come from rejection, generational, or some other way? If you have pride, you may not see it clearly.   You may be a narcissist, but can't see yourself this way. Ask God to show you. Humble yourself for God to work in you.

Notes:

Little Foxes That Spoil the Vineyard

Song of Songs 2:15 says?

Who is the vineyard?

From the book, give some examples of compromise, white lies and skeletons below:

Compromise:

-

-

-

-

-

White lies:

-

-

-

-

<u>Skeletons in the closet:</u>

-

-

-

<u>Laziness and procrastination:</u>
Give 3 examples of procrastination and the result of it.

1.

2.

3.

The Proverbs 31 woman in the Bible was classified as virtuous because of two main reasons, what were they?

1.

2.

The Proverbs 31 woman in the Bible was an example of a hard diligent worker. Give at least 5 examples of things she did to prove this (read the Bible passage to answer).

1.

2.

3.

4.

5.

<u>Idle (empty, inactive, lazy) time:</u>

The mind can be Satan's battlefield ___________________.

The mind needs to be protected by ____________________&
____

Idle time can give the enemy activity to __________________;

____________________; ____________________________

Philippians 4:8 says?

<u>Hypnosis:</u>
In short, what does the author say about your mind being a blank canvas?

What else can you say about idle time; inactivity of the mind or hypnosis?

<u>Mockery, ridicule or critical spirit</u>

Dictionary definition of contempt:

What is known as the "Golden Rule"?

Fill in the blank: See this sentence in the book. "You may not even be the mocker, but if you join in with others on the laughter and ridicule, you are an
______________________ which is just as bad."

Pray now against mockery and a critical spirit. Ask God to show you where it came from. Ask Him to forgive you.

<u>Judging/Bias:</u>

In brief, why were the Author 's guests short sighted regarding the restaurant event?

We can be bias, when we take sides with someone even when they're wrong. Are you bias when it comes to a friend, spouse, children? Who and why? Remember we need to stand up for the truth and justice regardless.

Luke 7:36–47 talks about? Focus on verse 39 and Jesus' response:

John 8:1–11 talks about? What is Jesus' response?

Explain in brief Romans 2:1-6

What's the main point in Romans 14:1-19?

<u>Swear / Curse words</u>:

Ask God to show you if you are unclean, angry or allowing your ear gates to receive whatever comes your way.   What's in your heart?   Matthew 12:34 says?

Briefly explain James 3:7-12

<u>Mean / unkind attitudes:</u>

Give all 9 of them from Galatians 5:22-23 –

______________________, _______________________, ______________________,

______________________, _______________________, _____________________,

______________________, _______________________, _____________________.

Finish this sentence from the book: "The way you treat people will bring a ________________ back to you."

Find the root, ask The Holy Spirit to show you. It may be rooted in rejections or bitterness and unforgiveness/ offenses. Repent from this behavior and ask God to change your heart.

<u>Selfishness / Narcissism:</u>

Give some synonyms to narcissism:

Define Narcissist -

Some symptoms of narcissistic personality disorder are:

A sense of self-importance.
Preoccupation with power, beauty, or success.
Entitlement
Can only be around people who are important or special.
Exploitative (unfair) for their own gain.
Abusive
Manipulative / Controlling
Arrogant
Lack of empathy
Must be admired

What would you change for more time with family?

Make time, because tomorrow is never promised and you will regret it.

Be honest with yourself; Do you operate in any of the above mentioned? If yes to even one of those, then you need to repent and ask God to help you break free. Ask God to show you every time you behave in this manner. Be transparent with God, because He already knows you anyway. Ask Him to show you where did it come from.

Take time to think about this section:
Are you neglecting spending time with your loved ones? If so, why? Is it selfish motives?

Notes:

<u>Tantrums:</u>

You use this to get what you want, *when* and *how* you want it. You are used to it. You may have attained things this way all your life. Do you use it together with anger?

Proverbs 29:22 says?

Proverbs 25:28 says?

Proverbs 16:32 says?

Where did it come from? Your parents, selfishness, a spirit of control and manipulation? Beware that it's not a Jezebel spirit.   Ask God to show you the <u>root</u> and to make you flexible and humble when you can't have it your way.   Be aware, because this is definitely not Godly and it's time to let it go!

<u>Notes:</u>

<u>Self-Pity:</u>

Fill in the blank from the book: Pity is not a ___________________ to the problem.

Self-pity is self-explanatory; it's SELF pity. No one else is dealing with your pity but YOU. God doesn't respond to SELF pity. This is not the way to get God's attention. The way to get His attention is reminding Him of His Word-Promises. Even if we don't have it together and we're a mess, He knows what to do with us, without a pity party. Ask God to help you stop this behavior. Ask Him now.

Notes:

<u>Don't look back:</u>

Luke 9:62 says?

What happened to Lot's wife based on this section of *Little Foxes*?

What happened to Abraham and Lot in Genesis 13?

Self-Reflection: <u>Who</u> do you have to let go of?   Someone that passed away; someone that left you; a business partner; a lover; family…

<u>What</u> do you have to let go of? A job; a city; a church; articles or items in your home; your past…

<u>Obedience is better than sacrifice:</u>

What did the Author learn regarding wearing the seat belt?

Define the word subtle; look it up:

Either from this section of the book or your own, give a few examples of _subtle_ rebellion:

1 Sam. 15:22 says?

Obeying even in the little things, is dear to God's heart. Ask the Holy Spirit to hold you accountable when you are operating in subtle rebellion. It's not only to protect you from open doors to the enemy, but remember that you get rewarded when you obey and do it God's way. Also, what are you teaching your children? Think about it.

Notes:

<u>God's name in vain:</u>

What does Exodus 20:7 and Deuteronomy 5:11 say:

A way that you use God's name in vain is when you say that "He said" or "He told you", but He didn't. Finish this sentence based on the book in this section: Beware, that we don't use His name for our personal ________________, __________________, or ____________________ because He will not hold us ____________________.

<u>Tithes and offerings:</u>

Bible says in Malachi 3:6–18:

Fill in the blank: Tithe is separate from the ____________________

What did God request of Abraham to sacrifice?
____

Fill in the blanks based on this section in the book: The offering should be given not just out of ____________________, but more out of ____________________.

Briefly explain Luke 18:18–24:

Why don't you tithe? Be honest with yourself.

YOU CAN'T AFFORD NOT TO TITHE!

<u>Poverty Mentality:</u>

Fill in the blank based on this section in the book: This mentality is not just about finances; it is a ________________________________ in many areas, especially lack of wisdom.

Are you putting your finances in order or even creating a budget? Today is a good day to start a real budget and view where your money is going. Hold yourself accountable or have someone hold you accountable. Create a budget now or ask someone to help you put one together.

A poverty mindset goes beyond the money. It's all about how you think. What is the "just in case" syndrome?

Based on this section in the book, fill in the 6 blanks: This type of mentality will allow you to lose your integrity and good morals. It is a state of mind that's ____________________, ____________________, ____________________, ____________________, ____________________, ____________________.

Remember to watch your confessions, as you have power of Life or Death in your tongue (Proverbs 18:21). Also, remember to be a cheerful giver (2 Corinthians 9:6-7 ESV - "Whoever sows sparingly will also reap sparingly, and whoever sows bountifully, will also reap bountifully. Each one must give as he has decided in his heart, not reluctantly or under compulsion, for God loves a cheerful giver").   Afterall, this is God's way and you will get what you've planted. God is faithful. Do it His way.

Be honest with yourself. Study this and see if you have a poverty mindset. Ask God to forgive you.

Notes:

<u>Prostituting:</u>

In short, what can you say about this in a non-sexual way?

Give your own example of how one can prostitute ourselves for money non-sexually.

<u>Prejudice:</u>

Based on this section in the book, Principalities of segregation exist and they come in with: _________________, _________________, _________________,

_________________, _________________, _________________,

_________________.

Be honest, have you battled with being prejudice, bias, bigot, chauvinist, macho, sexist, presumptuous, even arrogantly pious? If so, where did it come from? Ask the Holy Spirit to reveal its onset. Then repent from it and renounce it. Pray that God would break this off of your life and that you may catch yourself when behaving this way. You may have to ask others for forgiveness.

Notes:

<u>Holidays:</u>

Jeremiah 4:22 says?

Hosea 4:6 says?

2 Corinthians 2:11 says?

Go and do a study on *the origin* of some of the holidays we celebrate, you will be surprise at what you will find. You don't want to be ignorant of the devil's devices (tactics). We may not fit in with everyone; even if we stand out on our own, we are not going to go against God's ways or open up doors to the enemy.

"Enter by the narrow gate. For the gate is wide and the way is easy that leads to destruction, and those who enter by it are many. For the gate is narrow and the way is hard that leads to life, and those who find it are few." Matthew 7:13-14 ESV

Notes:

<u>Silence or isolation:</u>

We cannot expose ourselves to just anyone, but we do need to have
______________________.

We don't need to keep quiet for fear of what others might think or other's judgment. The key is to speak up and be free.

Based on this section of the book, give a few reasons why some men are angry:

Why is it important to talk to someone of the <u>same</u> sex based on the book?

Based on this section of the book, if you keep holding in, one day you'll explode the wrong way on the wrong people. If you hold in, you will ________________ because this is just like a slow ____________________.

Don't forget that forgiveness is key, even being able to forgive *yourself*. Make the time right now to go back to forgiving. Remember that if you failed a few times at something, it doesn't mean you're a failure, it just means you, like all of us, have weaknesses and have fallen short.

Ask God to show you and put your first and last name below for forgiveness:

______________________________   ______________________________

James 4:17 says?

Overall, what did you think of the *Rooted Issues* book?

Would you recommend it to others?

Would you help others, by doing your own group using the book and this Workbook?

Keep in mind, that these rooted issues are just to expose some things in your life that need to be uprooted for good. However, there could be so many other things. Also, realize that these are not total solutions to your problems, but they can be a start. The process can be lengthy; nevertheless, understand that God is in total control. He truly wants you free more than you do. *He whom the Son sets free, is free indeed!*

<u>Final notes:</u>

The following list is the one mentioned in the **<u>Chapter of Rejection</u>**. Do the list for at least 21 days consecutively and make it part of your life for the renewal of your mind.

<u>WHO I AM IN CHRIST</u>

I am…

A child of God……………………………………………………………………1 Jn. 3:1
Imperishable; incorruptible……………………………………………… 1 Peter 1:23
Forgiven of all my sins and washed in the blood of Christ…………Heb. 9:14; Eph. 1:7
A new Creation, the old has past and the new has come……………2 Cor. 5:17
The Temple of the Holy Spirit……………………………………………1 Cor. 6:19
Delivered from the domain of darkness into God's Kingdom………Col. 1:13
Redeemed from the curse of the law…………………………………Gal. 3:13; 1 Peter 1:18
Blessed and highly favored……………………………………………Gal. 3:9; Deut. 28: 1-14
A Saint; Pure and Holy…………………………………………………Rom. 1:7; 1 Cor. 1:2
The head and not the tail………………………………………………Deut. 28:13
Above and not beneath…………………………………………………Deut. 28:13
A Lender and not a borrower……………………………………………Deut. 28
The Healthy and not the sick……………………………………………Deut. 28
A chosen race; A nation of Holy People………………………………1 Peter 2:9
A Royal Priesthood (King & Priest or Queen & Priestess) …………1 Peter 2:9
God's own possession……………………………………………………1 Peter 2:9
Holy and without blame before Him…………………………………Eph. 1:4; 1 Peter 1:16
Elect………………………………………………………………………Eph. 1:4; Col. 3:12
Established to the end……………………………………………………Phil. 1:6; 1 Cor. 1:8
Close to God, through Christ's blood…………………………………Eph. 2:13
Victorious…………………………………………………………………Rev. 12:11; Rev. 21:7
Set Free – He whom the Son sets free, is free indeed………………Jn. 8:31-36
Strong in the Lord…………………………………………………………Eph. 6:10; Col. 1:11
Dead to sin, alive to God………………………………………………Rom. 6:2, 11; 1 Peter 2:24
More than a conqueror……………………………………………………Rom. 8:37
Joint heirs with Christ……………………………………………………Rom. 8: 17
Sealed with the Holy Spirit of promise…………………………………Eph. 1:13
In Christ, thanks to the work of God……………………………………1 Cor. 1:30
Accepted in the Beloved (Christ)………………………………………Rom. 14:3; 15:7
Complete in Christ………………………………………………………Col. 2:10
Crucified with Christ……………………………………………………Gal. 2:20
Raised with Christ, seated in heavenly places………………………Eph. 2:6; Col. 2:12
Free from guilt and condemnation……………………………………Rom. 8:1; Jn. 5:24

Reconciled to God...2 Cor. 5:18
Worthy to share in His inheritance.................................Col. 1:12
Firmly rooted, built up, established in my faith..................Col. 2:7
A fellow citizen with the saints, a member of God's household.........Eph. 2:19
Built on the foundation of the apostles and prophets;
Jesus is our Chief Cornerstone...Eph. 2:20
Just as He is.. 1 Jn. 4:17
Untouchable to the evil one..1 Jn. 5:18
Faithful to Christ...Rev. 17:14
Blessed with every spiritual blessing.. Eph. 1:3
His disciple, proved by my love for others............................ Jn. 13:34-35
The salt of the earth..Matthew 5:13
The light of the world...Matthew 5:14
The righteousness of God, because of what Jesus did.................2 Cor. 5:21
A partaker of God's Divine nature.. 2 Peter 1:4
Justified by faith through His blood...............................Rom. 3:24; 5:1
Sanctified (set apart) ....Jn. 17:17
Perfected by His one offering..Heb. 10:14
Foreknown by God...Rom. 8:29
Called of God... 2 Tim. 1:9
First fruits among His creation...James 1:18
Chosen by Jesus.. Jn. 15:16
An ambassador for Christ.. 2 Cor. 5:20
Precious to God – valued as the pupil of His eye.............................Deut. 32:10; Ps. 17:8
Healed by the wounds of Jesus...1 Peter 2:24; Isa. 53:6
Being changed into His image..2 Cor. 2:18
Love by God..Jn. 7:23; 16:27
An overcomer...1 Jn. 5:4
Hidden with Christ in God...Col. 3:3
A receiver of all that I ask in faith...................................... Luke 11:10
A finder of all that I seek in faith.......................................Luke 11:10
An enterer through doors God opens as I knock in faith.........................Luke 11:10
God's fellow worker... 1 Cor. 3:9
God's field... 1 Cor. 3:9
God's building.. 1 Cor. 3:9
A living stone, a spiritual house..1 Peter 2:5
A letter of recommendation from Christ.......................................2 Cor. 3:1-3
A minister of a New Covenant...2 Cor. 3:6
Glorified...Jn. 17:22
Unveiled; open; nothing to hide because of the Glory
He sheds through me..2 Cor. 3:16
One with Christ and my fellow believers......................................Jn. 17:21-23

I have…

Christ's life as my life...Col. 3:4
The mind of Christ; My mind is renewed daily...1 Cor. 2:16
An inheritance that will never diminish.....................................Eph. 1:11; 1 Peter 1:4
Access to the Father through the Holy Spirit...........................Heb. 4:16; Eph. 2:13
Everlasting life...Jn. 5:24; 6:47
The peace of God, which is beyond human understanding..............Jn. 14:27; Phil. 4:7
The power that raised Jesus from the dead...Eph. 1:19-21
The Greater One in me..1 Jn. 4:4
Everything that pertains to life and Godliness..2 Peter 1:3

Personal confessions:

I have…

The Power of Jesus
The Name of Jesus
The Authority of Jesus
The Blood of Jesus
The faith of Jesus
The love of Jesus
Positive confessions
Great wisdom, insight, discernment, understanding and revelation
Prosperity, as my soul prospers
Money; it comes from the North, South, East and West
Great boldness; I am fearless
Great favor
Great faith that moves mountains

My family (husband / wife - children) walk as one with God.
We learn to communicate.
We love each other.
We are united in harmony and peace.
My marriage is blessed or my future marriage is blessed.
My children are blessed.
Everything I touch prospers.
I lay hands on the sick and they recover.
God makes me willing and able.
I am obedient.

Contact Author Mayra Leon
www.mayraleon.org

Email: rootissues7@gmail.com

P.O. Box 10768
Brooksville, Florida 34603

Donate or purchase with

Cashapp: $jesuscares777
Venmo: @mleon14
PayPal: paypal.me/jesuscares
Zelle